J394.26546

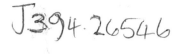

D0230171

EDUCATIONAL RESOURCE SERVICE

PERTH AND
KINROSS LIBRARIES

Celebrations!

Baisakhi

Mandy Ross

EDUCATIONAL RESOURCE SERVICE

PERTH AND
KINROSS LIBRARIES

Heinemann
LIBRARY

H www.heinemann.co.uk/library
Visit our website to find out more information about Heinemann Library books.

To order:
☎ Phone 44 (0) 1865 888066
🖹 Send a fax to 44 (0) 1865 314091
🖥 Visit the Heinemann Bookshop at www.heinemann.co.uk/library to browse our catalogue and order online.

First published in Great Britain by Heinemann Library,
Halley Court, Jordan Hill, Oxford OX2 8EJ
a division of Reed Educational and Professional Publishing Ltd.
Heinemann is a registered trademark of Reed Educational & Professional Publishing Ltd.

OXFORD MELBOURNE AUCKLAND
JOHANNESBURG BLANTYRE GABORONE
IBADAN PORTSMOUTH (NH) USA CHICAGO

© Reed Educational and Professional Publishing Ltd 2001
The moral right of the proprietor has been asserted.

All rights reserved. No part of this publication may be reproduced, stored in a retrieval system, or transmitted in any form or by any means, electronic, mechanical, photocopying, recording, or otherwise without either the prior written permission of the Publishers or a licence permitting restricted copying in the United Kingdom issued by the Copyright Licensing Agency Ltd, 90 Tottenham Court Road, London W1P 0LP.

Designed by Celia Floyd
Originated by Ambassador Litho Ltd
Printed by Wing King Tong in Hong Kong

ISBN 0 431 13796 X (hardback)
05 04 03 02 01
10 9 8 7 6 5 4 3 2 1

284464

British Library Cataloguing in Publication Data

Ross, Mandy
    Baisakhi. – (Celebrations)
    1. Baisakhi (Festival) – Juvenile literature
    I. Title
    394.2'6546

Acknowledgements
The Publishers would like to thank the following for permission to reproduce photographs:
Ann & Bury Peerless: pp6, 7; Christine Osborne Pictures: pp13, 14, 15, 19; Corbis: Gunter Marx p9, Dave Bartruff p16, Chris Lisle pp18, 20, Earl & Nazima Kowall p21; Format: p5; Impact: Mohamed Ansar p8; Trip: H Rogers pp10, 11, 17

Cover photograph reproduced with permission of Christine Osborne Pictures

Our thanks to the Bradford Interfaith Education Centre for their comments in the preparation of this book.

Every effort has been made to contact copyright holders of any material reproduced in this book. Any omissions will be rectified in subsequent printings if notice is given to the Publisher.

Contents

Words printed in **bold letters like these** are explained in the glossary.

Baisakhi

Baisakhi is the most important religious festival for **Sikhs**. It is celebrated in the middle of April, and marks the Sikh New Year's Day. In the Punjab (now part of India and Pakistan), where **Sikhism** began, Baisakhi is also the time of the harvest festival.

It was on Baisakhi day in 1699 CE that **Guru** Gobind Singh founded the **Khalsa**, or Sikh **fellowship**. So Baisakhi is also the birthday celebration of the Khalsa.

This map shows the Punjab where Sikhism began. Most Sikh families originally come from this area, although Sikhs have settled in many countries now.

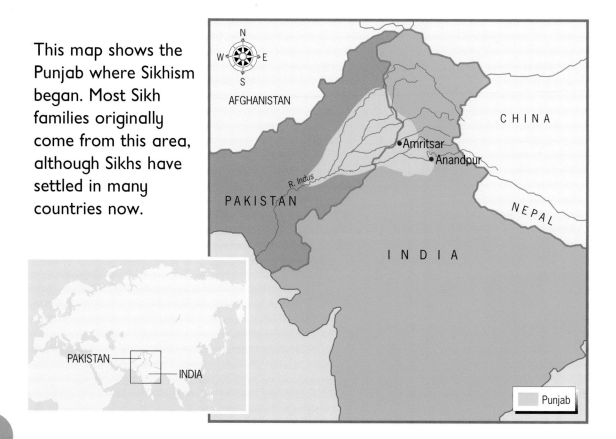

Baisakhi is a happy festival. There are prayers and celebrations at Sikh temples, or **Gurdwaras**, all round the world. Wherever they live, Sikhs organize joyful processions through towns and villages.

Afterwards, there is a mela or fair in the park, with food and drink, funfair rides, **bhangra** dancing and music, and fireworks after dark.

What do Sikhs believe?

Sikhs believe in one God, called Waheguru or **Akal Purakh**. They follow the teachings of the ten human Gurus, or teachers, and their **holy scriptures**, called the **Guru Granth Sahib**.

Joyful processions take place on Baisakhi day.

The story of Baisakhi

On Baisakhi, or New Year's Day in 1699, thousands of **Sikhs** travelled to the city of Anandpur in India. There they celebrated the harvest, and waited to meet their great leader, **Guru** Gobind Singh.

At last, the Guru appeared from his tent. He was dressed in a brilliant **saffron** yellow robe and a **turban**. But on this Baisakhi day, Guru Gobind Singh asked a strange and troubling question. 'Is there anyone here who will give their life for our God, **Akal Purakh**?' he said.

Everyone was silent. At last one man came forward. 'I will give up my life,' he said.

This is a picture of Guru Gobind Singh. Many Sikhs hang decorated pictures of the Gurus in their homes.

6

The man was taken by Guru Gobind Singh into the tent. There was a swish and a terrible thud, and then blood flowed out from under the tent. The Guru came out carrying a bloodstained sword. The crowd was horrified.

Again he asked the same question. After a long time, another man came forward. The same happened again and again until it seemed that five men had given up their lives.

The crowd was shocked. Could their beloved Guru have beheaded five innocent men?

A **gurdwara** in modern-day Anandpur.

The Five Beloved

Then, to the amazement and joy of the crowd, the five men followed **Guru** Gobind Singh out of the tent. Now they were wearing the same yellow robes as the Guru.

'These brave men were ready to give up their lives for their God!' cried the Guru. 'They are now the **Panj Piare**, the Five Beloved, soldiers and saints. They will become the first members of the **Khalsa**, the new **fellowship** of the Sikhs.'

Guru Gobind Singh with the Five Beloved, the original Khalsa.

The Khalsa today

The Khalsa is still an important part of the Sikh **religion**. It is a symbol of the Sikh belief in equality and working together. Sikhs can become a member of the Khalsa through a special ceremony called **Amrit**, which often happens at Baisakhi. For more about Amrit, see pages 12–13.

Members of the Khalsa in a modern procession. They are carrying traditional curved swords.

The ten Gurus

At the heart of the **Sikh religion** are the teachings of the ten **Gurus**, or teachers. Guru Nanak, the first human Guru, began teaching around the year 1500 CE. All the Gurus taught the importance of justice, equality and **fellowship**, or community.

Guru Gobind Singh was the last of ten human gurus. He was born in Patna, in India in 1666 CE. He taught his followers to be strong and to fight for justice and for their beliefs. He formed the **Khalsa** on Baisakhi day to strengthen the Sikh community.

A traditional painting showing the ten Gurus. The eighth Guru, Har Krishan died of smallpox when he was eight years old. Schools are often named after him.

The holy scriptures

Guru Gobind Singh taught that after his death, there would be no more human gurus. Instead, Sikhs should follow the teachings of the **holy scriptures**, called the **Guru Granth Sahib**. It contains poems written by the Gurus in Gurmukhi, a form of the Punjabi language.

The Guru Granth Sahib is treated with great love and respect, as if it were a person.

A Sikh woman reading the Guru Granth Sahib.

The Five 'K's and the Amrit ceremony

Guru Gobind Singh told his followers to wear five signs to show that they were **Sikhs**. They are known as the Five 'K's, and many Sikhs still wear them.

These are the Five 'K's:

Kesh – uncut hair. Many Sikh men wear a **turban** as a sign of respect for God

Kangha – a wooden comb to look after your hair

Kara – an iron or steel bracelet

Kirpan – a sword, symbolically worn by the Khalsa as a symbol of strength

Kachera – cotton shorts, usually worn under clothes to show modesty.

The Five 'K's.

Amrit ceremony

The **Amrit** ceremony is held at the **Gurdwara** on Baisakhi day. Sikhs can take part in the ceremony at the age of 14 or over. They promise to keep strictly to the Sikh **religion**, and join the **Khalsa**.

Wearing the Five 'K's, they drink amrit, and then it is sprinkled on them. The Amrit ceremony is a solemn but happy time.

The Khanda

The **Khanda** is the symbol which appears on the Sikh flag. In the centre is a double-edged sword, which stands for one God, who can create as well as destroy. The circle is called a chakkar. A circle has no beginning and no end, so it reminds Sikhs of God.

This is the Sikh flag, showing the Khanda. It is always yellow, the colour of saffron.

At the Gurdwara

On Baisakhi day, many **Sikhs** go to the **Gurdwara**, their place of **worship**. There they join in prayers and services, which may last all day. The Gurdwara is crowded and joyful.

In front of every Gurdwara there is a flagpole where a flag called the Nishan Sahib flies at all times. The flag bears the **Khanda**, the Sikh symbol. The flagpole is dressed in orange robes.

Everyone helps to raise the flagpole on Baisakhi day.

Each year at Baisakhi, the flagpole is lowered so that the flag and the robes can be removed. The flagpole is washed with yoghurt, which Sikhs consider to be very pure. Then everyone helps to raise the flagpole again with new robes and a new flag flying from the top for another year.

Gurdwaras are built to honour the Sikh **religion**. There are some beautiful Gurdwaras in India and Pakistan, and in Britain, too. But many Gurdwaras are very simple. Sometimes an ordinary house is used for worship.

This beautiful Gurdwara is in Hounslow in London.

Food to share

In every **Gurdwara** there is a large kitchen, called a langar, which means 'the anchor'. People work together in the langar to make food to share, so that nobody goes hungry.

Everyone, old or young, male or female, can help to cook. This is a way of working for the community, which is an important part of all the **Gurus'** teachings.

Sikhs sharing a meal at the Gurdwara. They sit in long, straight lines as a reminder that everyone is equal before God.

How to make karah parshad

Karah parshad is a special food that is shared at the end of prayers in the Gurdwara.

You will need:

1 cup sugar	1 cup wholemeal
1 cup melted butter	flour or semolina

1. Put the sugar with some water into a pan. Simmer until the sugar dissolves.
2. Mix the butter and flour in another pan and fry till the flour is golden brown.
3. Add the sugar water to the flour and stir over a low heat until the mixture becomes very thick.
4. Leave to cool and set for at least half an hour.

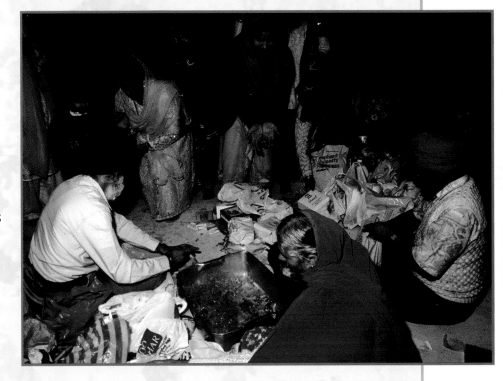

Sharing karah parshad. Everyone bows and cups their hands to receive a portion.

Celebrations: bhangra dancing...

Bhangra dancing was originally a farmers' dance in the Punjab, in India. Groups of men would perform it on Baisakhi day.

The dance tells the story of a farmer's life. The dancers pretend to be carrying tools to the fields where they dig and sow. They look up to the sky and pray for rain. At last the rain comes and the farmers are happy. They circle around, stamping and clapping, faster and faster, until the dance ends in a mad whirl.

Bhangra dancers in traditional costume. Bells worn on their ankles ring as they dance.

...and music

Music is an important part of **Sikh** culture and **worship**. The **Gurus'** poetry is sung to music, called kirtan, and everyone can join in the singing in the **Gurdwara**.

Sikh children are encouraged to learn to play traditional instruments such as the tabla or dholak, which are different sorts of drum. The harmonium is another popular instrument. It was brought to India from Britain.

Playing the harmonium (on the left) and tabla drums.

Punjab, where Sikhism began

The name 'Punjab' means five rivers. It is fertile land where Hindus, Muslims and **Sikhs** once lived side by side. But in 1947 **CE** the modern states of India and Pakistan were formed, and Punjab was split. Many Sikhs went to live in the Indian part of Punjab. (See the map on page 4.)

The Golden Temple, or Harimandir Sahib, at Amritsar in Punjab is the most important **Gurdwara**. The very first copy of the **Guru Granth Sahib** was brought there in 1604.

The Golden Temple at Amritsar. The temple is decorated with about 162 kilograms of gold.

The Golden Temple is built in the middle of a pool. Sikhs believe that bathing in the pool can heal people who are sick.

Baisakhi is a great festival in the Punjab. People flock to the Golden Temple and other Gurdwaras for prayers and singing, and to share food in the langar. There are huge melas, or fairs, where people come to enjoy themselves.

Sikh men celebrating in Punjab.

Sikh festival calendar

Guru Nanak's birthday

To celebrate **Guru** Nanak's birthday, in November, the **Guru Granth Sahib** is taken on a procession on a specially decorated float. The Five Beloved lead the procession, followed by people carrying flags and banners.

Divali

Divali, the Indian festival of light, falls in October or November. At Divali, Sikhs remember Guru Har Gobind who saved 52 imprisoned princes. They light candles and fireworks, and **Gurdwaras** are lit up with hundreds of coloured lights.

Hola Mohalla

Guru Gobind Singh wanted his followers to be fit and strong in case they were attacked. So he started the spring festival, Hola Mohalla, with archery competitions, wrestling and other sports. Young Sikhs are still encouraged to take part in sports.

EDUCATIONAL RESOURCE SERVICE

Glossary

Akal Purakh one of the Sikh names for God

amrit sweetened holy water or nectar. The Amrit ceremony is named after it.

CE Common Era. People of all religions can use this, rather than the Christian AD, which counts from the birth of Jesus Christ. The year numbers are not changed.

fellowship a group of people who share aims or beliefs

Gurdwara Sikh place of worship

Guru a Sikh religious teacher and leader

Guru Granth Sahib the Sikh holy scriptures

holy respected because it is to do with God

Khalsa the Sikh fellowship

Khanda the Sikh symbol, made up of swords and a circle

Panj Piare the Five Beloved ones

religion belief in God or gods

saffron a spice that gives a bright yellow colour to food. Saffron can be used as a dye, too.

scriptures writings contained in a book

Sikh someone who follows the Sikh religion. The word Sikh means 'learner'.

Sikhism the religion of Sikhs

turban head-covering worn by Sikh men and women, made from a long cloth wound round the head

worship to show respect and love for God

Index

Titles in the *Celebrations* series include:

Hardback   0 431 13796 X

Hardback   0 431 13790 0

Hardback   0 431 13793 5

Hardback   0 431 13791 9

Hardback   0 431 13794 3

Hardback   0 431 13795 1

Hardback   0 431 13792 7

Find out about the other titles in this series on our website www.heinemann.co.uk/library